GEORGE WASHINGTON

False Wooden Teeth

THE HISTORY HOUR

Copyright © 2018 by Kolme Korkeudet Oy

All rights reserved.

No part of this book may be reproduced in any form or by any electronic or mechanical means, including information storage and retrieval systems, without written permission from the author, except for the use of brief quotations in a book review.

CONTENTS

PART I
Introduction   1

PART II
Growing Up to Be Great!   5

PART III
What Could or Would George Do Now?   13

PART IV
George Takes A Wife   27

PART V
George Becomes a Mason?   35

PART VI
What Was George's Tie To The Stamp Act,
Townshend Acts, & The Continental Congress   39

PART VII
Revolutionary War, 8 Long Years   45

PART VIII
George Retiring? From What? Farming? Military?   61

PART IX
George Has Doubts He Can Lead The Nation   65

PART X
George Elected First President – 1789   69

PART XI
George and God   97

PART XII
No Looking Back – On to Mt. Vernon   101

PART XIII
Strengths   107

PART XIV
Weaknesses   109

PART XV
Conclusion   113

Your Free eBook!   117

❧ I ❧
INTRODUCTION

෴

As we grow up in school and study the presidents, we learn of course who our First President was that served the United States. We keep in our mind for some reason as we grow and get older that George Washington wore false wooden teeth and that is why you never see a picture of him smiling. The explanation sounds good when you are a child, and at that time you can't refute that story.

෴

As you get older, you learn about the political system we live in today and odd as it may seem, the majority of it we pick up by osmosis because we sure don't seem to listen carefully to what the news is telling us unless it has been given to us as an assignment for that evening.

※

We all think that when we were young that politicians were noble, but since the beginning of time, maybe that has not always been the case. Instead, they too have cheated and maybe lied their way to the top just as they do today.

※

The difference is social media, wiretapping, up to the minute news reporting, and hidden security cameras that look like buttons and light switches that can record anything that is said up to 200 feet away with pure clarity.

※

In this version, you will find things about George Washington that might surprise you and that you did not know before you read this book. You will find out that he was the type of man that tried to lay things out in such a way as to make his opponent look bad or if need be, to bend the truth if necessary. It is about the boy who was not supposed to tell a lie about chopping down a cherry tree, but when it came to war and the presidency, telling the truth did not always serve him well, so it was better to make up a fictional fabrication to keep himself out of trouble.

※

You will still not have every answer to every question you might want to know about this man. In some ways, he was an exciting man, deep thinking and quiet, while in other ways, you will be able to make many comparisons to the way our government is projected now in the fake news and what the press tells us is supposed to be factual reporting on our government.

※

I guess it is true that there is nothing new under the sun.

※

I am one that still believes in the inherent goodness of man. Somehow, that seems to be getting dimmer with every birthday that comes along. In its place comes the shrewd but hateful side of people who will sell out their own country for some fool's gold.

❧ II ☙
GROWING UP TO BE GREAT!

"Guard against the impostures of pretended patriotism.'

— GEORGE WASHINGTON

۞

Most people in George Washington's time started out life in the same way. You were either very poor, lower middle class, or extremely rich.

۞

George Washington, however, was one of the lucky kids of his generation. He was born into money on February 22, 1732. His family was not the richest by any means, but they were considered very comfortable and had a large family plantation on Pope's Creek located in Westmoreland County, Virginia.

※

George's great-grandfather migrated to Virginia from England. They were a family of "***distinction***" in the old country and henceforth were granted land by King Henry VIII.

※

During the Puritan revolution, George's grandfather lost most of their family's wealth.

※

His father, Augustine Washington lived from 1694 to 1743, and he was married to his second wife, Mary (Ball) Washington who lived from 1708 to 1789. Mary was 14 years younger than her husband, but she lived 46 more years after his death.

※

During their marriage, they had six children, and five of them survived childhood which was extremely unusual for that time.

※

While George was growing up, he never lacked for children to play with and it made no difference to him as to the color of their skin. At Pope's Creek, George was surrounded by every farm animal one could imagine such as chickens, dogs, pigs, cows, and horses.

※

When George turned three years old, Augustine decided it was time to move the entire family to a much larger plantation farther north up the Potomac that was known as Little Hunting Creek. It was in what is known now as Fairfax County in Virginia.

※

A few years later when they moved again, and for the last time, it was to be near Augustine's iron mine, he was so vested in at Accokeek Creek, which is today known as Stafford County and lies on the Rappahannock River. It was called the "***Ferry Farm,***" and this was what George would always consider his childhood home. They were recognized as moderately prosperous middle-class folks.

※

If it's true that George did cut down that cherry tree, then it probably happened here at Ferry Farm. George's childhood was spent sailing on the river, hunting and fishing, and swimming. What more could a boy ask for while he was growing up?

※

George went to a small school for a time in Fredericksburg and took practical subjects that were required for everyone. But what he aspired at was subjects like math and draftsmanship which would serve him well as a great land surveyor.

༺❀༻

The knowledge that George gained in everyday life would bode well for him just by knowing the backwoods people, the plantation foremen, and he also learned the art of growing tobacco, surveying, and raising stock.

༺❀༻

George had been away visiting a cousin that lived not too far from Ferry Farm when he received by messenger an urgent note to come home as fast as he could get there. The letter said his dad was dying. It is not precisely known, but it could have been exacerbated by pneumonia, but when they ruled the official cause of his death, it was "***gout of his stomach.***" Augustine died on April 12, 1743, at the age of 49 years old.

༺❀༻

Lawrence being his oldest son by his first marriage, in Augustine's will, he left him the Little Hunting Creek. Lawrence would rebuild this home and rename it, Mount Vernon. To George, his part was left in trust with his mother until he came of age and he would inherit the Ferry Farm and all its surroundings.

༺❀༻

His father's death had an impact on George that no one will ever realize.

George's mother Mary never remarried and felt George should have the title as head of the estate, but it didn't seem to matter because she still supervised everything. George preferred the company of his half-brother Lawrence who lived at Mount Vernon and Fairfax children at the Belvoir Estate.

George did become a surveyor and quite a successful one at that. For his profession, he went on many expeditions, and it led him to go into the Virginia wilderness, and it was there that he learned the area. George earned enough money that he was able to start buying up land.

In 1748, George turned 16 years old and traveled with a group of surveyors in the western territory of Virginia, learning the trade and working along the side of men who were experts at the craft.

In 1749, with the aid of Lord Fairfax, George was appointed to be the official surveyor for the County of Culpepper.

For the next two years, George would remain busy surveying in Culpepper, Augusta, and Frederick counties. The experience alone helped toughen his mind and body, and become a very resourceful man.

He started to become interested in land holdings out west, and that seemed to remain with him throughout his entire life as he purchased land in that direction.

In 1751 Washington went on a trip with his half-brother who was older than he, outside of America. It was George's first and only trip out of America's borders. He and Lawrence traveled to Barbados. Lawrence had been suffering from tuberculosis, and they hoped by going somewhere the climate was warm he might recuperate.

They had only been in Barbados for a short while when George contracted dreaded smallpox. George survived, but smallpox left his face covered in scars.

In 1752, George's mentor and half-brother, Lawrence who had received his education in England, died. It was only two months later that Lawrence's only child, Sarah, died. Washington now found himself without his father and his friend and mentor, Lawrence.

Eventually, George would be the one to inherit Lawrence's estate, on the Potomac River, Mount Vernon. George was twenty years old at the time.

◊✹◊

No matter what happened to him in life, George would always feel that farming was one of, if not the most honorable professions a man could pursue.

◊✹◊

George would eventually work to increase his acreage to about 8,000 acres.

❦ III ❧
WHAT COULD OR WOULD GEORGE DO NOW?

"Observe good faith and justice toward all nations. Cultivate peace and harmony with all."

— GEORGE WASHINGTON

※

It was the early 1750s; Britain and France seemed to be at peace. But the French Military started sneaking in and occupying more and more of the Ohio Valley supposedly to protect the King's interest in the land and watch over the fur trappers and what was going on with the French settlers.

※

It seems that the death of George's brother Lawrence had left a vacancy for the post of Adjutant General. It was then that George decided to stop surveying land and begin to be a soldier, pursue the position because he was inspired by Lawrence's previous service to Admiral Edward Vernon.

※

In December 1752 he was assigned to a less-distinguished District in the Southern part of the Colony of Virginia by the Lieutenant Governor at the time Dinwiddie. Then, Fitzhugh resigned as the District adjunct of the North and George lobbied for that position. He was appointed the position in February 1753 and was going to receive an annual payment of 100 pounds. He accepted the appointment of British Ambassador for the Military to French Officials and the Indians that reached north as far as Erie, Pennsylvania. George was 21 years old in 1753.

※

Washington had seemed to be showing "*early*" signs of leadership that appeared to be natural for him and shortly after Lawrence died, Lieutenant Governor of Virginia, Robert Dinwiddie, made George the Lieutenant Colonel in the militia of Virginia.

※

It was October 1753 on Halloween that Dinwiddie sent George to Fort LeBoeuf. Today it is known as Waterford, Pennsylvania. He was to warn the French to leave the land that had been claimed by Britain. The French said they were not going to go anywhere so George rode as fast as he could back to Williamsburg.

※

Dinwiddie then sent George back, only this time with troops and they set up an encampment at the location of Great Meadows. George led a party of about forty men all night long as they marched forward to where the French were positioned. At dawn, this small group spotted the French and attacked the post. Shots were being fired, and the firefight was non-stop in that wooded wilderness.

※

George's group killed thirteen of the French soldiers and took twenty-one more as prisoners. It seems that George got his first thirst for blood at this battle, wanting the taste more and more each time he would go to battle. Both sides wanted to claim that the other side fired upon them first, but the bottom line was this battle sparked a war that spread around the world to Africa, Europe, and India. It was the beginning of the French and Indian War.

※

The French drove home a counterattack and pushed George, and his men back into their post in Great Meadows also called Fort Necessity as it was built in the middle of the meadow, causing it to be in a poor location and vulnerable if a fire started in the nearby woods that encircled the field. It was after this full day siege on July 1, 1754, that George gave up and surrendered, and he was soon released.

※

George signed what appeared to be a falsely translated document of surrender that stated he had been "***assassinated***" in Jumonville, and this mistranslated confession that was false became what they used to blame George for starting the war.

❦

Historian, Joseph Ellis feels this episode revealed George's initiative and bravery, but it also glaringly showed his carelessness and inexperience. When George got back to his home state of Virginia, George refused to take a demotion in his rank down to captain and therefore resigned his commission.

❦

George was somewhat embarrassed to be captured but was glad to receive a thank you from the House of Burgesses and see in the London Gazettes where his name had been mentioned.

❦

Though he had lost on all counts, George was a mere aide-de-camp volunteer who was unpaid and answering to Edward Braddock instead of what he felt was his militia rank.

❦

He felt subordinate to the junior officers and was subjected to embarrassment. He could taste receiving a Royal Commission so much that the went to Boston to see Governor Shirley that had taken over as commander in chief when General Braddock died.

❦

George did not succeed in getting what he went after, but Governor Shirley issued a decree for officers that served in the militia in Virginia that they would outrank any of the British officers that were lower in rank in 1755.

※

This army was to capture Fort Duquesne. Their march of the troops was beginning to slow down as it proceeded forward, and George told Braddock that he thought they should divide the army into two parts – one, a primary column, and a more lightly mobile and equipped "***flying column***" as their offense.

※

In this Battle, the French along with their Indian friends ambushed the divided forces, and mortally wounded the general. The British were in trouble. They had suffered a severe number of fatalities and started retreating in a panic with at least two-thirds either injured or killed.

※

Washington, who had a fever and a headache and was recovering from dysentery, but managed to get what was left of his troops organized, and they retreated. During this battle, he lost two horses that had been shot out from under him, his coat and hat both were riddled with bullet holes. The British loss was 977 that were either wounded or killed.

※

For this one act alone George was given the title of "***Hero of Monongahela***" by Governor Dinwiddie, who also changed

George's rank to Colonel over the 1,200 man Regiment of Virginia. To some, it seemed that his conduct under fire might have redeemed his reputation at this point among the critics in his command that had been in the Battle at Fort Necessity.

※

When it came to the new Commander Colonel Thomas Dunbar when he was planning the new force movements, he did not include George, possibly because of Georges' recommendation of the flying column formations that had turned out so badly.

※

August 1755 rolled around, and Dinwiddie gave George the reward of naming him Colonel of the Virginia Regiment as well as Commander in Chief of any forces raised that defended His Majesty's Colony. It came with the task of protecting the frontier of Virginia.

※

The Virginia Regiment became the first non-British military unit, full-time formed by the new colonies and George was told to "***act offensively and defensively***" and do what he thought best.

※

George was happy to get the commission, but he wanted a red coat that the higher ranking officers wore so badly he could taste it, and it continued to escape his grasp. With that, so did the pay that with which came with that commission. Why George desired the salary seems to elude this author's understanding as he was already the owner of several acres of farmland and had been acquiring more as he surveyed land and acquired more as he continued to work.

※

Dinwiddie tried to get the British group to include the Virginia Regiment with its ranks, but no way would they let this happen. George was so sure that Braddock would recommend him for the commission in the British Army, that George asked Lord Loudoun.

※

Loudon told him, "**NO**" and instead he transferred the responsibility for Fort Cumberland to the state of Maryland, and this freed up Virginia's Regiment of most of its duty, and this unnerved one angry George Washington.

※

Washington had to command over one thousand men, and he was such a disciplinarian that believed in training. He led his troops in brutal campaigns, and they fought 20 battles in ten months time, and he lost one-third of his men. It seemed to be Georges only unqualified success during the time of the French/Indian War.

※

If one was thinking rationally, it was an easy decision. The troops had already struggled to come through the central

Pennsylvania wilderness, and all were sick, poorly fed, and deserting at a fast pace. It was hard to get provisions in because of the rough road that had been cut through the forests and then over the four ridges of the Alleghenies that was between Forbes' and Ligonier supply base in Carlisle, so in winter they would not be able to get supplies.

※

They could not get a good idea of the number of hostile Indians that were at Fort Duquesne. They were not even sure of the size of the garrison at the French fortress. Also, if they could take over the fort, they did not know if they could hold it all winter. The attack was delayed until after winter passed.

※

It took only two weeks to realize that the situation around Forbes' army had undergone a dramatic change and that Forbes' expedition would be the one to stand out.

※

The real reason for this war was for nothing less than who would maintain control of the fertile Ohio River Valley, and the real struggle was between the French and British. Today, on this site, is where the Monongahela River and the Allegheny River meet in the city of Pittsburgh.

※

It was at Great Meadows that George Washington attempted to obtain a foothold for Virginia on July 4th, 1754 when a

French force that had been based at Duquesne that made him surrender at this poorly located Fort Necessity.

※

So, trying again, in the summer of 1755, there was a British force led by General Braddock who set out to seize Fort Duquesne. Braddock's army, moved along the north by the Monongahela River, got ambushed and routed, its leader killed on July 9th.

※

The British colonials in Pennsylvania were beginning to panic and started sending letters to Philadelphia, letters to one another, telling of the terror that was sweeping through their counties like a wildfire, and trying to get their leaders to please send them soldiers and to build forts for them. Governor Robert Hunter Morris of Pennsylvania could do little to help.

※

November 11, 1758, Brigadier General John Forbes decided to call together a council of war where else but at his headquarters at Fort Ligonier that was about 40 miles due east of what was then considered the French stronghold, Fort Duquesne. He had a distinguished group of experienced battle-hardened men. Among them were, Sir John St. Clair, Henry Bouquet, Archibald Montgomery, George Washington, William Byrd, John Armstrong, James Burd, and Hugh Mercer.

※

He had about 6,000 men to make up his army that was poised to strike Fort Duquesne and winter was upon them and could trap his army up in the Allegheny Mountains. Forbes had to decide as to whether to advance now on that French fortress or settle down for the winter and wait until the spring came.

※

It would not be until late in 1758 that the British finally came up with a strategy to reverse the tide. The British planned on attacking the French at Louisbourg, Nova Scotia, drive them out of the Champlain-Lake George area in New York by grabbing Fort Carillon; and then get rid of the little chain of forts that ran south of Lake Erie down to Fort Duquesne. If this feat was to be accomplished, they felt they would need Brig. Gen. John Forbes to oversee the provincial and British expeditionary force.

※

Forbes building a road caused two difficulties that proved to be significant. No one was sure how they would be able to clear the way through the mountains to get 6,000 soldiers through and then manage to bring in a steady stream of supplies to those soldiers.

※

The second difficulty was that the Virginians were being led by no other than George Washington who did not want Pennsylvania to open any roads leading into the Ohio territories. It was a sore point with Virginia as it caused a significant dispute inside Forbes' group and almost undermined his plans.

※

The soldiers all started getting sick with stomach and respiratory infections. Even Forbes' officers would be stricken and bedridden for days at a time. Forbes, having been trained as a physician knew he was dying and only lived until March 11, 1759. Forbes, who realized he had the '***bloody flux,***' was dehydrated, blinded by migraines, terribly constipated, and could barely walk to the point he could not get out of bed. It seemed even to the end, as ill as he was his mental capacity, remained intact.

※

There were multiple small units from here and there representing different factions, but there were two Virginia Regiments that were commanded by George Washington and William Byrd.

※

Forbes's group was often riddled by the desertion of their soldiers, those that stayed were drunk all the time and were behaving ridiculously. Washington would at times conspire against Forbes ideas to finish a new road. Those actions would be to the point of getting rid of General Forbes himself.

※

When one reads Washington's old letters, it reveals his anger about Forbes' constant refusal about their incessant arguments. In one such letter, George complained of how much time had been wasted. He felt that Forbes probably did not have orders for some of the things he carried out.

George wrote that if it were necessary, he would travel to the planned Virginia mission to England to let the king know just '***how much the Public's money had been misused.***' George was not mincing words; he finished his letter by saying he could prove what the truth of the mission indeed was, as he had taken more pain than anyone else to get to the bottom of this disgrace.

When Forbes found out that George was going behind his back, he said that George was unfit for duty and Forbes was furious. He had seen through George's planned maneuver that would only advance Virginia and its claim to all the western territory and keep Pennsylvania from claiming its own.

George Washington tried to learn from his mistakes since one of his letters had landed in the hands of Forbes, but Forbes continued to ignore George's arguments to use the Braddock road. All evidence seems to suggest that Forbes went forward to carry out his orders with due diligence.

Forbes big problem was the man he had chosen to oversee provisions and logistics, St. Clair could not get along with anyone. No matter who he encountered, he seemed to alienate them as soon as he met them. His problems of being nice to others started with bureaucrats and farmers, then continued to his fellow soldiers.

※

When it came to it, the French met George Washingtons group. There is an anonymous account in the Pennsylvania Gazette on November 30, 1758, that state during the battle that part of Forbes' group upon hearing the action of the conflict hurried through the early morning hours to help Washington and his group. They were soon being shot at by the soldiers they were coming to help (friendly fire if you will). Before anyone figured out what was happening, there were 14 Virginians killed.

※

The British still scored a significant victory, captured Fort Duquesne and took control of the Ohio Valley.

※

It was considered this war and the battles involved were won due to the abilities of General Forbes. Even though Forbes had to struggle with great difficulties and maintain his armies in a seeming wilderness and marched them over almost what one would consider impassable mountains and through thick woods; his actions required that of experience and foresight. Considering how ill he was and that he was able to surmount all of these problems and was still able to drive the French out of Ohio and blow up their Fort. The French and their reign in the United States were gone forever.

※

In December of 1758, George said he had had enough, he resigned from his commission, went back to Mount Vernon totally disillusioned and retired. He felt his experience during his time in the war was just plain frustrating, as decisions were made too slow, there was weak support from the legislature, and the recruits were so poorly trained it was pitiful.

IV
GEORGE TAKES A WIFE

"It is far better to be alone, than to be in bad company."

— GEORGE WASHINGTON

After George left the army, he married one Martha Dandridge Custis on January 6, 1759. Martha was a widow, 28 years old, and was a few months older than he. Martha came to their marriage with considerable wealth. Martha being a gracious woman; she was also intelligent and extremely experienced in managing a farm estate, so it made for a harmonious marriage.

She had an 18,000-acre **"estate,"** and George purchased 6,000 acres of it from her. After buying this land, and with what land he already had, and along with what he had earned for his military service, George was one of the top landowners in Virginia.

※

To this marriage, Martha brought her two young children. John (Jacky) who was six years old and Martha (Patsy) who was four. George could not help but lavish affection on both of them.

※

Since George was never able to have any biological children, he was happy to have two children to raise.

※

When Patsy was about eleven or twelve, she started having seizures caused by epilepsy. George and Martha consulted several doctors and tried every cure they heard about, but nothing worked for poor Patsy. During this time in history, there were no anti-seizure medications. Even during the 1700s, it was not normal for anyone to die from epilepsy. Patsy had lots of seizures after they started, but she always recovered from them just fine.

※

It was June 1773, and Patsy was talking to her **"about to be sister-in-law,"** Eleanor Calvert at Mount Vernon. Patsy had gone to her room to gather a letter that Jack had sent her while he was away at college.

Eleanor heard a weird sound and found Patsy lying on the floor in her bedroom in the middle of a seizure. George and Martha were called to the bedroom immediately. George picked her up and laid her on her bed.

In family letters, it describes George at Patsy's bedside, kneeling, with tears running down his face, asking God for her to recover. In two minutes, Patsy was dead. They buried her the next day. George wrote to his brother-in-law that Patsy his

"innocent, sweet, girl had passed away."

He goes on to say that Patsy had eaten dinner that afternoon and was feeling better than she had in a long time. This time when she had a seizure she died within two minutes and did not utter a groan, a word, or a sigh. It was unexpected and sudden, and Martha is very depressed.

By reading George Washington's account of Patsy's death, it is undoubtedly one of the best and earliest descriptions of **SUDEP** (Sudden Unexpected Death in Epilepsy). It is still not known how it causes death. It seems to be the typical pattern for death in the young that are between the ages of 20-40. They are generally in excellent health except for the fact of their seizures. Most of the time it happens at night and goes unwitnessed. Families usually find them prone in their beds or at least near their beds. **SUDEP** is rare; you will see that it strikes one out of 1,000 to 3,000 people who suffer from epilepsy every year. If death is going to be considered **SUDEP**, there can be no other reason for the cause of death.

The next day George wrote a friend:

> *"It is easier to conceive, than to describe, the distress of this family, especially that of the unhappy Parent of our dear Patsy Custis when I inform you that yesterday removed the sweet, innocent girl into a more happy and peaceful abode than any she has lived with, the afflicted path she hitherto has trod."*

George canceled anything to do with business and did not leave Martha for a single night for three months. Patsy's death did enable him to get rid of the British creditors since he did inherit half of her inheritance.

Then Jacky passed away during the Revolution. He was serving as a civilian aide to the camp for George Washington during the time of the Yorktown Siege. Unfortunately, Jacky Custis came down with "***camp fever,***" which in today's time would be referenced as dysentery. Custis died November 5th, 1781.

❦

When Custis died so young at age 26, his wife (widow) let her two youngest kids live with George and Martha for them to raise. When this happened, George immediately adopted both of Jacky's children, Eleanor Parke Custis and George Washington Parke Custis. Martha and George were never able to have any children of their own, and it is thought that maybe his bout with smallpox left him sterile.

❦

When George married Martha, he became one of the wealthiest men in Virginia, and it did help his standing socially. He gained control of one-third of Martha's 18,000 acres which was worth $100,000, managed the remaining for Martha's children, and since Dinwiddie had promised land to the soldiers in the French and Indian War, George acquired 23,200 acres more to add to his 8,000 acres from his brother Lawrence.

❦

In 1783, Custis's widow remarried a Dr. David Stuart from Alexandria, Virginia and had 16 more children.

❦

Even though Custis was well-established when he died, his financial arrears were in such a mess due to his poor business decisions and the wartime taxes that after he died in 1781, it took administrators over ten years in negotiating an end to the final transaction over the purchase of Abingdon. It did not entirely liquidate until 1811 when his widow died. His four children then inherited over 600 slaves.

※

After George retired from the Virginia militia and until the start of the Revolution, he made his priority developing his land, managing his livestock, rotating crops, and trying to keep up with the latest in scientific advances.

※

George loved being the farmer and being out on his horse overseeing his land. He enjoyed fishing, fox hunts, and cotillions. He was working six days every week. You would find him out with his coat off working beside his hired hands. He bred his horses and cattle and tended to the fruit orchards he owned.

※

He kept over 100 slaves, and it is said that he did not believe in slave ownership, but then again accepted the fact that the law was for slavery. It is difficult for this author to understand if he was indeed against slavery why he kept slaves. Why did he not free them and pay them as laborers?

※

During this time, George got his first taste of politics when he was elected to the House of Burgesses of Virginia during 1758.

※

George was a '***respected***' landowner and military hero; he held a local office and was elected to the Virginia legislature. He represented his County at the House of Burgesses for a total of seven years starting in 1758. When it came election time, he filled the voters up with beer, hard cider, brandy, wine, rice punch totaling 170 gallons – all while he was away on the Forbes expedition. There were three other candidates, and he won the election by about 40 percent of the vote.

***

During these years George made sure he positioned himself as a political figure and social elite in the state of Virginia. For over eight years he would invite 2,000 guests to join him at his Mount Vernon home, most of them being "***people of taste and rank.***" If people were not among the elite social status, he would treat them civilly but made sure to hold them at a proper distance, so that they could get to know him. In 1769 he became more active in politics when he tried to get the Virginia Assembly to pass an embargo on any goods coming from Great Britain.

***

Washington lived a lavish type lifestyle. His favorite hobbies were dances, fox hunting, parties, races, theater, and cockfights. He liked playing backgammon, cards, and billiards. George imported the fine luxuries and whatever goods he wanted from England and to pay for them, he exported his tobacco crop.

***

When 1764 rolled around, all the luxuries and the tobacco

market being weak, he found himself 1,800 pounds in debt which in today's times would be $2,359. He had a lot of holdings, but no liquidity, no easy cash. He decided to bolster his solvency by paying more attention to his money, diversifying his business, and not ordering so much from England. He changed his cash crop to wheat from tobacco, so that he could process the wheat in its various forms in the colonies. He kept diversifying his operations, and it would include fishing, milling flour, hog production, horse breeding, weaving, and spinning. It would be twenty-six years later when he would build a distillery for making whiskey that would produce 1,000 gallons each month.

❦

Of significant note, in 1779 fall, George inspected the lands that had been given to the veterans of the French and Indian War. He surveyed the land and was given the best of the acreage anywhere on the tract. George told the other veterans that their land was no good as it was unsuitable for farming and he would buy it from them. It was a total of 20,147 acres. Most of the veterans seemed to be happy about the sale of their land while there were others that realized they had been duped. (For someone who believed for justice for all, this was a mean thing to do to others who had fought with him.

V
GEORGE BECOMES A MASON?

"To be prepared for war is one of the most effective means of preserving peace."

— GEORGE WASHINGTON

George was only 21 years old when as a young Virginian he became a Master Mason which at the time was to be considered the highest of the basic rank in this secret fraternity of what they called Freemasonry. Due to the decline of cathedral buildings or "***lodges***" as they were also called it was decided to admit those who were not stonemasons to increase and maintain their membership. It allowed the secret fraternal order to grow even more in popularity in Europe.

The first Masonic Lodge in the American colonies was built in the city of Philadelphia in 1730 and the future leader of the revolution; Benjamin Franklin was one of the founding members.

☙❧

Freemasons are each governed by their local order's many rites and customs. Their members can trace their origins of the Masons all the way back to the building of King Solomon's Temple in the Bible, and all of them are expected to believe in the "***Supreme Being,***" to follow certain religious rites, and to keep a vow of secrecy when it comes to the ceremonies conducted in their meetings.

☙❧

Of note, the Masons of this time adhered to what was considered liberal democratic principles that would include loyalty to the government and religious toleration.

☙❧

The Free Mason's seemed to encounter lots of opposition from the organized religious faction, and most of it from the Roman Catholic Church.

☙❧

George considered it another feather in his hat, a showing of his civic responsibility. When he became a Master Mason, George could go through a series of rites that would let him "***rise***" in status in the Masons. Right before he became president of the United States, George had been elected as the first Worshipful Master of Lodge No. 22.

※

There were leaders who had fought in the American Revolution that were Free Masons. Some of them were John Hancock and Paul Revere of the Boston Tea Party. The Masonic seal can be seen on the design of the seal on the one-dollar bill. It is the All-Seeing Eye above a pyramid unfinished with the scroll beneath it that states "***New Secular Order***" in Latin. This seal began showing up on the one-dollar bill during Franklin D. Roosevelt's presidency who was also a Mason.

※

Today, Freemasonry is still playing an important role in United States politics, with at least 15 presidents, five Justices on the Supreme Court, and Congress that have numerous members of Masons.

VI
WHAT WAS GEORGE'S TIE TO THE STAMP ACT, TOWNSHEND ACTS, & THE CONTINENTAL CONGRESS

"Discipline is the soul of an army. It makes small numbers formidable; procures success to the weak, and esteem to all."

— GEORGE WASHINGTON

The British Government decided to play ugly and imposed a "***Stamp Act***" on their American Colonies. Taxpayers in Britain were already paying a Stamp Tax, and the state of Massachusetts had already dabbled with a similar type law, but what was required of the residents living in the colonies was above what already existed. Britain was trying to raise the money they felt was needed to provide military expenses for the colonies.

❦

The law was passed on March of 1765, but it was not to go into effect until November of 1765.

❦

There was so much resistance to this tax that the protests around it were called the Stamp Act Crisis. The Stamp Act Congress repealed the said stamp act.

❦

The Stamp Act - was soon noted as an economic and political failure for Britain. The realization soon came that the colonies knew they needed to begin to organize the efforts to be rid of Britains power.

❦

The Townshend Acts – In the colonies there were four acts that Britain had passed attempting to exert its authority over the American colonies. They tried by suspending a stubborn representative assembly and came up with strict ideas for collecting revenue duties. The colonists named this set of acts after the man who sponsored them, Charles Townshend. It all happened between June 15- July 2, 1767.

❦

Suspending Act – it kept the New York Assembly from being able to conduct any more business until it complied with all of the financial requirements for the Quartering Act to address the expenses of the British troops that were stationed in the American colonies.

※

Townshend duties – it enforced a direct revenue duty. That means money aimed not merely at trying to regulate trade but to put money in the British treasury. You needed to pay at the colonial ports, and the duties were on tea, paper, glass, and lead. It would be the second time for the colonies that they had a tax forced on them to raise the revenue.

※

Third Act – It established some strict and mostly capricious machinery of collections regarding customs in the American colonies. It would include the searchers, officers, coast guard vessels, spies, writs of assistance, search warrants, and even a Board of Customs Commissioners in Boston. It was all to be financed from the customs revenues.

※

Fourth Act – it lifted the commercial duties that were in place on tea, letting it be exported to the American colonies free from Britains taxes.

※

The four acts were an immediate threat to what had been traditions already established by the colonies as self-government, mainly the practice of taxing through representing the provincial assemblies.

All the acts were repealed March 5, 1770, except for the one dealing with tea. By lifting the acts, it seemed to avert hostilities temporarily.

Then came the Boston Massacre on the same day the acts were repealed. Five colonists were killed by British regulars. It culminated tension between the American colonies and the British troops that had been there to enforce those tax burdens.

The trial had some interesting aspects in that the Captain and the eight soldiers trial was the longest so far in the colonies history. It was the judges the first time to voice **"*reasonable doubt.*"** There was Benefit of Clergy that was used in this trial by two of the soldiers that helped them to escape the penalty of death.

The Intolerable Acts played a specific roll in causing the American Revolution.

To guide the American Colonies from 1774 to 1789, it would be the Continental Congress. It was to be considered as the first government of the thirteen American colonies.

In the year 1776, the Continental Congress declared that America was independent of Britain. It would be five years later that Congress would pen and ratify its first national constitution and the Articles of Confederation. The country would use these documents to be governed until 1789 when it would be replaced with the United States Constitution.

VII
REVOLUTIONARY WAR, 8 LONG YEARS

"If the freedom of speech is taken away then dumb and silent we may be led, like sheep to the slaughter."

— GEORGE WASHINGTON

When the fighting broke out in April 1775, George showed up at the meeting of the Second Continental Congress wearing his military uniform. He wanted Congress to know he was ready for war. George wanted everyone to know he had the military experience, the prestige, the military bearing, the reputation of a staunch patriot, and he felt the people of Virginia supported him.

George was not there on purpose to seek the office of commander and told them he was not equal to, or even up to it, but, there was no other competition for the position.

※

Congress formed the Continental Army on June 14, 1775; John Adams nominated George to be appointed as the Major General and the Congress elected him to be the Commander-in-Chief.

※

When George left his home in Mount Vernon, he would not be back for more than six years. In the winter, it seemed the months would drag on forever, and fighting between the colonies and the British would come to a standstill. It would be during this time George would ask Martha to be with him wherever he was stationed.

※

Poor Martha, every year when the winter came she would make the hard trip to get to his camp, no matter where it would be. Martha would stay with him for months on end. Usually, during the entire time of the war, Martha was able to be with George about half the time he was away from Mount Vernon.

※

Martha was liked by the Patriots, but the loyalists hated her. Some of the people were afraid she would be kidnapped and then be used for leverage against George.

※

Martha helped with the war effort in that she would raise money for the Patriots to help purchase items like food or uniforms for the soldiers. Martha donated over $20,000 of her own money for the war effort.

※

Before Martha could ever go to the winter camps with George, she had to undergo being vaccinated for smallpox. At that time in history, smallpox was one of the deadliest diseases a soldier could encounter while at war and highly contagious.

※

While with him, Martha worked as George's secretary and entertained guests. It seemed by her being there it would boost the morale of the troops and her husband.

※

In July of 1775, George took over his command at Cambridge, Massachusetts in the heart of the siege of Boston. He walked into an army that was in desperate shortage of gunpowder, his soldiers poorly outfitted, poorly sheltered, and a group that was undisciplined, so he asked for new sources.

※

George started reforming the men he had to work with by drilling his soldiers, and he imposed strict discipline that included fines, floggings, and even incarceration. He told his officers they should get to know their men and to help their recruits understand the military duties that were best suited for each soldier, they were to respect civilians and to be reading their military manuals. Anyone who was a coward was gone.

He had to get gunpowder for his men. British arsenals were raided, there was an attempt to manufacture some, and a little bit of supply was gathered toward the end of 1776, most of it from France.

Washington restructured his army during the standoff and made the British withdraw by placing artillery at the top of Dorchester Heights that overlooked the entire city. The British got out of Boston immediately, and George moved his group of men to New York City.

Britains newspapers were always against the Patriots in the Continental Congress, but for some reason, they were still praising George Washington for his qualities and personal character as a leader and military commander.

Both sides in Parliament seemed to find George's endurance, courage, and attentiveness to his troop's welfare worthy and excellent examples of what they wish they had in their commanders. George refused to get involved in the politics. Instead, he stayed focused on his mission to his men.

※

In August of 1776, British General William Howe hurled a massive land and naval campaign that was designed to take New York and then bargain a settlement.

※

Under George Washington, the Continental Army fought the enemy for a first time army as the Independent United States for the thirteen colonies; it was to be the biggest battle of the war.

※

It was and the British having several more victories caused George Washington to hightail it with his men out of New York and into New Jersey. They threw caution to the wind, and it placed considerable doubt as to just how stable the Continental Army really might be.

※

Of all the famous pictures one remembers, it is the one of George Washington crossing over the icy Delaware River. It was sundown, the lousy weather was getting much worse, and a light rain had started falling. On that night George Washington led his men to cross the Delaware River, moving 18 heavy pieces of artillery, working against fast currents and ice blocking their way. Because of the weather, George had divided his troops into three divisions, but only one made it across the raging, icy river that night. The other two made it across the next morning in heavy snow and sleet.

※

Christmas Eve night 1776, George Washington decided to attack by leading his men across the icy Delaware River and capturing almost 1,000 Hessians in New Jersey.

※

He then went on to Princeton in early January. The winter time victories raised his group's morale, secured George's position as a leader, and made every young man in the world want to join the armed forces.

※

In February George and his men stayed in New Jersey and he felt sure that all of his troops needed to be vaccinated against smallpox so he would not lose any more of his troops.

※

September 1777 there was a skirmish between the British and Washington's men in Philadelphia that was much too complex for George's men who were less experienced and they had to accept defeat.

※

While this was happening, there was the Battle of Brandywine, and George's men tried to attack the British garrison at Germantown in the early part of October, but they were not to be so successful.

※

When the British Burgoyne was forced to surrender his entire group at Saratoga, France decided to enter the war, by being an ally to America and this act turned a Revolutionary War into what would be a World Wide War.

※

George's losing in Philadelphia caused some of the Congressmen to start discussing removing George from his post. When they tried to do this, it failed due to George's supporters standing up for him.

※

It seemed at this point that the admiration for George was starting to wane, and on top of this John Adams was not giving him any credit.

※

It happened that George's army stayed at Valley Forge during December of 1777 and stayed there for six months. During winter, out of 11,000 men, the group lost 2,500 to 3,000 of them to exposure, the right clothing, inadequate shelter, lack of food, extreme cold, and disease.

※

The British were paying for their goods with sterling and were living well in Philly. George, on the other hand, suffered terribly in getting the supplies he needed with American paper money depreciating. The food source of wild game from the nearby woodlands was exhausted. When February rolled around, George had to face the enormous task of keeping morale up and discouraging desertion.

George had asked over and over from the Continental Congress for the provisions that were so desperately needed but he met with total resistance. Due to his urging, in January of 1778, there were five Congressmen that came to examine just how bad the conditions were at Valley Forge. After this visit, Congress backed George with full support and expedited the process. By the end of February, George's men had everything they needed.

When spring arrived, the army seemed to emerge in good shape, in part due to a training program that had been supervised by a veteran of the general staff of Prussia.

There was one thing that George was ever wary of, and that was to always be on the watch for espionage, and he developed a system that he would be able to identify British plans and their locations.

George usually being on top of situations that involved betrayal seemed to be looking the other way when it came to incidents of disloyalty of the one and only Benedict Arnold who was his trusted Army Officer. Benedict had shown himself well in many battles, and George had come to trust him and depend on his skills.

Benedict had been injured during a battle and could no longer ride horseback into combat. Because of this, Benedict was talked "***into***" by his '***loyalist-leaning***' wife to meet up with a merchant by the name of Stransbury so Benedict could defect to the British.

Arnold could sight several reasons he was angry and was prepared to commit treason against his country. He was furious because he had been passed over for promotions that were given to officers under him and it made him mad at Congress; he had been war profiteering, and if caught Benedict could very well face a court-martial; and have to pay back all he had stolen. There were no clues that the British had come looking for him to betray his country. It seemed clear he was set on deserting his country.

Starting in the summer of 1780, Arnold began his nasty plot. He kept the information highway open to Andre' with as much sensitive information he could get his hands on that would cause problems for George Washington so the British could take over West Point. Benedict kept aggravating George for promotion and George finally made him the commander of West Point.

※

It came September 21st, 1780, and time for Benedict to meet Andre' Stransbury out on the banks of the Hudson River where Benedict gave Andre' the plans so the British could overtake West Point. Andre' took the plans and hid them down in his boot.

※

Two days rolled by and Andre' was caught by army officers who found the plans hidden in his boot. Reinforcements were sent just in case to ensure that West Point would be safe and secured.

※

Benedict, knowing full well what had happened, took off on horseback (remember if you will, before now, his battle injuries had kept him from being able to ride a horse), he boarded a sloop that was waiting for him and managed to escape.

※

When George found out he had gotten away, he was livid and immediately brought in every commander that had answered to Benedict as a precaution. At this point, George had no idea that Benedict Arnold's wife was involved in this terrible plot. George took over command of West Point, and this caused the British to give up hope, and they never tried to take over West Point again.

※

When Benedict Arnold got off the sloop in New York, he was paid by Clinton for his betrayal and was named a senior British commander fighting patriots in Connecticut and Virginia.

※

Andres' trial by a military court was for spying, and he was sentenced to death. George Washington tried to trade Benedict Arnold for Andre,' but the British turned down the offer. Andre' asked George to let him be killed by a firing squad. George started to grant that request but changed his mind so he could make an example of a traitor. Andre' was hanged in New York, October 2nd, 1780.

※

In 1778, the British left Philadelphia and went to New York, but George and his army launched a full attack on them at Monmouth and pushed them off the battlefield. The British kept heading toward New York. George then moved his group of men to the outskirts of New York.

※

In the summer of 1779, under George's direction, General John Sullivan was sent to retaliate for the Tory and Iroquois

Indians attacking American settlements early in the war. They carried out a mission that they called "***Scorched Earth***" crusade that demolished about forty Iroquois Indian settlements along with their crops in upstate New York.

※

For the winter 1779 – 1780 George decided to settle his troops in Morristown. It would be the troop's worst exposure to the elements yet during the war. They suffered temperatures of 16 below. The ground was frozen over with ice and snow for weeks on end, and again the troops were without provisions.

※

The final blow was in 1781 when the French Navy win allowed the French and American armies to trap a British Legion in Virginia.

※

It was seventeen days after the successful Siege of Yorktown that Jack Custis would no longer be among the living. He had joined George Washington as a volunteer aide at the camp specifically for this one campaign. Jack had contracted the ever famous "***camp fever***" which covered any number of illnesses. The disease was causing him to fail fast. Jack had wanted so badly to see the surrender that faithful comrades lifted Jack on his stretcher so he could see all of the proceedings. It was probably the most significant achievement of George Washington's life to this point.

※

To try and save Jack's life, they moved him 30 miles to Eltham Landing in Virginia, where one of his uncle's, Burwell Bassett, owned some land and had a plantation. They called his wife, Eleanor and his mother, Martha to come to his bedside.

☙❧

Before George Washington could be with Jack, Jack slipped away on November 5, 1781. It was the last of Martha's children that she had birthed. Martha went into a "***solemn and deep distress.***" George Washington held Jack's widow and told her that he felt that Jack's two kids were the same as if they were his own.

☙❧

George and Martha would take over raising Jack's two youngest children. Jack's widow, while leaving the two children with Martha and George, would by the time the war was over be remarried to a Dr. David Stewart and they would have a family of sixteen children.

☙❧

October 17, 1781, the surrender at Yorktown, ended most of the fighting. George was known for his accomplishments in this war, but George suffered several defeats before attaining victory.

☙❧

March 1783 was upon them, and George Washington did

everything he could to diffuse a situation with a group of Army '***officers***' (the Newburgh Conspiracy) who said they were going to confront Congress about their back pay. They wanted their money and wanted it now.

※

In September 1783 the Treaty of Paris was signed that would declare the United States as Independent and free of Britain.

※

George Washington dispersed his men, then on November 2nd, 1783 said goodbye to his soldiers with a farewell address. November 25th, 1783 the Brits left New York City, and then George and the governor took ownership.

※

December 4th George told his officers goodbye, he had led the Continental Army for 8 ½ years; and then on December 23rd, 1783, he turned in his notice that he was resigning as commander in chief.

※

It was in the Senate Chamber in Maryland that George made a statement to the Continental Congress where he said,

> *"I consider it an indispensable duty to close this last solemn act of my official life, by commending the interests of our dearest country to the protection of Almighty God, and those who have the superintendence of them, to His holy keeping."*

During this period in history, the United States was following the Articles of Confederation and were without a President. It was to serve as the forerunner to the United States Constitution.

VIII
GEORGE RETIRING? FROM WHAT? FARMING? MILITARY?

"Truth will ultimately prevail where there is pains to bring it to light."

— GEORGE WASHINGTON

※

When George retired, he went back home to Mount Vernon, but his retirement was to be short-lived. He was interested in what the western frontier held, so in 1784 he went on an exploratory expedition. He checked out the land he had been granted as payment for serving in the French – Indian War.

※

He was persuaded to present himself at the Constitutional Convention in the City of Love, Philadelphia in the summer during 1787 as a representative of Virginia. While there, he was elected to be president of the Constitutional Convention.

George was critical however of the Articles of Confederation for what seemed to be a weak central government as he referred to them as no better than "***a rope of sand***" to hold a new nation together.

George felt there should be a strong federal government due to all the years he was so frustrated with British officials not being able to provide for their military when they so desperately needed supplies. The general consensus did not feel the same as George Washington because they thought a federal government would become more dictating like the British they had overthrown.

George did not debate much, he participated in the voting for and against the different articles, but with George's prestige it helped maintain cooperation, and the delegates kept their noses to the grindstone. When the delegates were designing the presidency, they did so with George Washington in mind and asked him to define the office of President of the United States.

After the Constitutional Convention, George's support

caused many, even the Virginia legislature, to go ahead and vote for approval; the new United States Constitution was then approved by all thirteen states.

※

The electors that represented the states under this new Constitution would vote for their new President February 4th, 1789. The official count would be delayed to wait until Congress achieved a caucus in New York, George Washington was suspicious that most Republican electors did not vote for him.

❦ IX ❦
GEORGE HAS DOUBTS HE CAN LEAD THE NATION

"True friendship is a plant of slow growth, and must undergo and withstand the shocks of adversity, before it is entitled to the appellation."

— GEORGE WASHINGTON

❦

The Inauguration was supposed to be held March 4th but had to be delayed because Congress could not meet the quorum before April 6th.

❦

Washington did win the election, unanimous in each state. John Adams came in second and therefore was elected as the vice president.

❦

Bear in mind the electoral college was set up entirely different at that time. Each elector was able to vote twice (what a mess that must have been). Maybe that was due to there only being thirteen states.

❦

There was a delay in certifying the election which made more time for doubts as George considered what the task would be like if he were elected. George enjoyed this period of waiting like it was a vacation; if he were elected, he was sure it would feel like he was being led to his execution.

❦

George loved his peaceful life at Mount Vernon. He always felt that he was not smart enough to be the president. The 13 colonies faced what he called an "***ocean of difficulties.***" While writing a letter to his friend, Edward Rutledge, he expressed the fact that he felt the Presidency was about the next thing to a death sentence. He felt his private life would never be the same again.

❦

There were 72 electors, and everyone but three voted and each elector could vote two times. George Washington appeared on every ballot of the 69. Almost half the electors cast their second vote for John Adams, who was named vice president. The rest of the votes went to 10 other candidates who were running for president.

The electorate college was nothing then to what it is now. The popular vote remains the same, however.

❦ X ❧
GEORGE ELECTED FIRST PRESIDENT – 1789

"When we assumed the Soldier, we did not lay aside the Citizen."

— GEORGE WASHINGTON

※

The day after the electoral votes had been counted and Washington was declared the first president; Congress told Charles Thomson, secretary of Congress to ride to Mount Vernon and notify him of his presidency.

※

I am sure that Thomson was not looking forward to making the trip to Virginia to tell George that he had been elected President. He was going to face bad roads, terrible weather, and wide rivers he would have to cross; broad rivers that may be deep.

It was okay with him though because he felt that Washington would be almost "***a father and a savior***" to get the colonies on the right track. Washington considered Thomson to be an exemplary patriot and a faithful public servant.

April 14, 1789, George opened the main entrance door at Mount Vernon and embraced his visitor, Mr. Thomson. After entering Mount Vernon, Thomson read the proclamation to George Washington that he was now the new President of the United States.

George did not feel he could meet the tasks laid out for the requirements of the job description for president. He said he knew the work itself was arduous and since it was laid at his feet he felt unable to rise to the occasion. He told Thomson that all he could do was try his best and go at the job with honest enthusiasm. This job in front of him was not like anything he had ever attempted in his entire life. All the aspirations for a republican government now lay in his hands. Before this turn of events, he had been able to stay in a cocoon of silence, but with this presidency, there would be nowhere to hide, and he would be continuously exposed to public scrutiny as never before.

Since the vote counting had been delayed for so long, George who was 57 years old, was starting to feel the crush of what was to come from the public affairs that would be left up to him. For this reason, he decided to set out as soon as possible for New York the morning of April 16th. With him came Thomson in George's elegant carriage and his aide, David Humphreys. He had written in his diary, and it gave way the sense of dread he felt:

> *"About ten this morning I said goodbye to Mount Vernon and my private life, to domesticity, and my mind feels so disturbed to the point that I am ever so anxious that I am having pain, more pain than I can express. I start my journey to New York, with my best intention to give my best service to my country and answer the call to which I have been assigned, but continue to feel little hope about meeting everyone's expectations."*

※

As he left, it was Martha that stood there waving goodbye to George. She would not join him until the middle of May. She watched as George started his journey. It was a bittersweet feeling as she wondered if he would ever come home to Mount Vernon. She had doubts about him taking on this public job, but I guess it couldn't be avoided. Martha felt their whole family would be dysfunctional, so she must get there as soon as she could follow him.

※

So George could travel quickly, he and his group started out every morning at sunrise and traveled all day. He wanted to keep distractions to a minimum, which he soon found was going to be impossible. He foresaw eight long days of partying ahead of him.

※

George had only journeyed a mere ten miles toward Alexandria when he has intercepted with a dinner that was prepared, and the lunch was drawn out by 13 mandatory toasts. Washington was a professional when it came to saying goodbye. His response to the townspeople was that he bid them all as being his kind friends and neighbors a goodbye.

※

It was soon realized that this trip would form a Republican equivalent to that of a procession leading to a royal coronation. George acted like he had been a politician forever as he left political promises all along the route. While George was in Wilmington, he spoke to the Delaware Group that Promoted Domestic Manufacturers. It was there he gave a hopeful speech. George told them he wanted to promote domestic manufactures, and with his plan, it would be one of the first issues to be expected to come from the new energetic government.

※

Arriving in Philadelphia, the town dignitaries met him and asked him to ride into town on a white horse. He came to a bridge to cross over the Schuylkill River and found it had been wrapped with evergreens and flowers. A little boy wearing a flower crown on his head and looking cherubic was lowered by a mechanical device, to place a flower crown on George's head. Everyone was chanting

"Long Live George Washington."

☙❧

When George entered Philadelphia, he found himself in front of a grand parade with 20,000 people along the sides of the streets, with their eyes watching him in astute wonder. Church bells were ringing as George continued to one of his old hangouts, the City Tavern.

☙❧

The next day, George was so tired of all the partying that when the light horse troops showed up to escort him on to Trenton, they found George had left the city an hour before them to stop the pomp and circumstance.

☙❧

When Washington neared the bridge that spanned Assunpink Creek in Trenton, the exact spot where the Hessians and British had been held back by him, he noticed the townspeople had made an elegant and beautiful arch made of flowers to honor him.

☙❧

As George came closer, 13 young girls, robed in white, walked toward George with baskets full of flowers as they scattered their petals at George's feet. He was sitting on his horse with tears standing in his eyes. He bowed to the young girls. The three rows of unmarried ladies, women, married ladies, and young girls burst into song about how he had saved them. All this admiration only made George doubt himself more.

※

George hoped he would be able to enter New York unnoticed and quietly. He had pleaded with the governor to please have no celebrations as he was ready for some peace and quiet.

※

He was crazy if he thought this would happen. When he had made it to Elizabethtown, New Jersey, April 23rd, he noticed three senators, three state officials, and five congressmen waiting for him. He had to have an idea that this welcome would be over the top compared to those in Trenton and Philadelphia.

※

There was a special barge, tied at the wharf, freshly painted and built in his honor, equipped with red curtains for an awning at the back so it would protect him from the elements of the weather. The craft was being steered by 13 oarsman wearing white uniforms.

※

As George's barge started drifting out into the Hudson, he could make out a shoreline of Manhattan that was "***full of a vast number of citizens all waiting with exultation for his arrival.***" Many ships were in the harbor anchored and decorated with banners and flags for George Washington.

༺༻

When George's Presidential barge pulled up to the wharf of Wall Street, there was Mayor James Duane, Governor Clinton, and James Madison along with other dignitaries who welcomed him to the fair city. George told everyone that for now, he would go along with this plan, but this needed to be over soon.

༺༻

The streets were solid with people and George to get to his new house at #3 Cherry Street; it took him one-half hour to get there because of the crowds of people.

༺༻

It was noted that George's attitude changed on his way to his new home as he gave in to the mood of everyone's high spirits, and it seemed especially so when he noticed the numerous adoring women. Washington was continually bowing to everyone and always taking his hat off to the women looking out their windows. The women were waving their hankies and throwing flowers and crying tears of congratulation and joy.

༺༻

The new Constitution did not call for a speech at the inauguration. George had been thinking about this even before he had been elected and asked David Humphreys to draft one for him. Humphreys turned out a speech 73 pages long. The address was a little on the ridiculous side due to George spending so much time defending why he decided to run for president.

༺۞༻

Fortunately, this speech was not given. Madison then helped George write a more compact speech. Madison would be there to help George in whatever way he needed. Madison became George's advisor and true confidant. It was odd that Madison was never bothered that in his relationship with Washington, it might somehow become interpreted as a violation of the balance of powers.

༺۞༻

George realized that all that he would do at the inauguration and swearing in would set the tone for America's future. Since it was the first time in the nations new future, it would set a precedent. He told Madison that he religiously hoped on his part that the examples would be founded on true principles.

༺۞༻

George would not wear his uniform to the inauguration, but he did wear a brown double-breasted suit that had been designed from broadcloth. The suit was adorned with a sanctified button that bore the symbol of an eagle on each one. He wore white hose, yellow gloves, and shoe buckles of silver. To polish off his image as President, George powdered his hair and put on a dress sword that had been sheathed in a scabbard made of steel.

༺۞༻

George Washington's inauguration was held where Nassau and Wall Streets interconnect in a building that for a long time had been used as the City Hall for New York. In September of 1788, Pierre-Charles L'Enfant remodeled the building into what was called Federal Hall making it the perfect home for Congress to reside. There was a covered arcade located at street level and on the second story a balcony. George would step out on this balcony and take his oath of office. Historians feel that it being the first inauguration was NOT by any means a pomp and circumstance affair but instead a slapdash affair. The preparations for the inauguration were rushed, and work on the building went on until just days before the big event. A couple of days before the inauguration, the eagle was placed upon the pediment, and that would complete the building. The building was white and topped by a white and blue cupola with a weather vane on top.

※

It would be a little after noon April 30th, 1789, and after listening all morning to prayers and church bells that a team of troops riding on horses would accompany carriages filled with legislators that would stop in front of George's new residence on Cherry Street to escort him to the inaugural site.

※

The processing trailed at a snail's pace as it went through the Manhattan streets and stopped 200 yards from their destination, Federal Hall. When George stepped off the carriage, he walked through soldiers who had formed a double line to enter the building where the members of Congress were waiting for him. When George entered, he bowed to each house of the legislature to show his respect.

⁂

The room became extremely quiet. The new Vice President, John Adams stood to give the official greeting and told George that this moment in time was upon him. He said the House of Representatives and the Senate were ready to give him the oath of office that the Constitution required of them. Washington let them know he was prepared to begin.

⁂

When George stepped out onto the balcony, there was a deafening roar from the crowd below. People were everywhere they could squeeze on the streets and every rooftop. George acted modest, stately, and it had a profound effect: he placed a hand over his heart and bowed to the crowd several times. Because of George's integrity, dignity, and his prior unrivaled sacrifices he had given to his country, he was a success with the people.

⁂

Congressman Ames from Massachusetts stated that time had already reeked havoc on George's face, and he already looked careworn and haggard.

⁂

Just that morning before the inauguration the Congressional committee wanted to add that George lay his hand on the Bible while he took the oath. A Masonic lodge provided a deep brown, thick, leather Bible that lay on a crimson velvet cushion. When it was time for the oath to be taken, the Bible lay on a table that was covered in red.

Chancellor Robert Livingston executed the oath to George Washington. George seemed visibly moved. When George had finished his oath, he bent over, picked up the Bible and lifted it to his lips. It is not known for sure, but legend has it that George added,

"So help me God."

It seemed to onlookers that George Washington was feeling this experience to the depths of his soul.

The crowds watching could not hear a thing, and Livingston had to raise his voice to notify the crowd below that the oath was finished.

With this part of the ceremony finished, George went to the Senate to give his inaugural speech. Congress stood as he entered the room and after Washington bowed in response, everyone sat down.

George seemed very nervous when he started his speech. His voice though deep was a little shaky and so soft everyone had to pay close attention so they could hear what he was saying. George seemed embarrassed and agitated at the same time.

When he gave his speech, he spoke of his anxieties about not feeling fit for the job as he thought he had inferior endowments by nature and no practice in civil government affairs. During his speech to Congress, he told them that he did not want to be paid, but Congress ignored his request and gave him an annual pay of $25,000. The one thing George did know was that "***God***" had been the overseer when it came to the birth of America. George went on to say that no one can be forced to acknowledge and worship the invisible hand of God, which does conduct the lives of men, more than the citizens of the United States. George may have been referring to the fact that he was feeling much older. He told those present that Mount Vernon was his retreat from the rest of the world.

George did not go into matters of policy but did cover the ideas that he would use to govern his administration. The first and foremost being national unity. George was careful that he did not endorse any specific religion. There was so much riding on his attempt to have a republican government.

After giving his speech, George led a procession up Broadway, to attend an Episcopal service at the Chapel of St. Paul's. After the devotions, George finally had a chance to relax for a short while.

That evening, the lower Manhattan area was covered in shimmering lights. Washington watched the fireworks for two hours. Finally, George could rest and get on with his new job as President of the United States.

※

It did seem that George was excellent at delegating and made a reasonable judgment with people of character and talent. He was out and with his staff and talking regularly with his department heads and would listen to what their advice was before he made a final decision.

※

He seemed orderly, systematic, solicitous of others opinions, energetic, decisive, but he was intent on the general goals and the actions it would take to achieve them.

※

George Washington, now President believed there should be a strong Presidency. Since he was the first President, that meant he could set several new rules, basically play the office by ear. George felt it was essential to work closely with his staff and he relied heavily on the advice of his cabinet members.

※

George was popular, and that was no doubt, Congress did not try and challenge any of his appointments to his cabinet. It was this principle that set Presidents to be able to get approval for their cabinet appointments unavoidably.

※

While George was serving his first term, he was forced to deal with significant problems. The old Confederation did not have the powers to handle its load of work. There was weak leadership, and part of it was because there was no executive, and only a small number of clerks; but they had a massive debt, no powers to tax, and paper money that was utterly worthless.

※

George had to face the fact that the United States was still not unified because Rhode Island and North Carolina had yet not joined the new Union, and the status regarding the independent Vermont Republic was still uncertain.

※

George was burdened with bringing together an emerging executive department; and he leaned heavily on Tobias Lear, his personal secretary, to help him with this selection.

※

Congress assembled the executive departments during the first few months of Washington's term in office, and it included the Department of War, The State Department, and the Treasury Department. Two additional officers were chosen without having departments, and they were the Attorney General – Edmund Randolph and the Postmaster

General – Samuel Osgood. George also appointed Thomas Jefferson from Virginia as the Secretary of State, Secretary of War would be Henry Knox, and Alexander Hamilton he picked for the Treasury Department.

※

In 1791 Hamilton and Jefferson got into a huge argument that went public because of the nosey newspaper the "***National Gazette.***" The fighting got so bad that Jefferson went to George Washington and told him that Hamilton's system would totally undermine and probably overthrow the Republic.

※

Hamilton believed there should be a strong federal government that needed a Federal bank backed with Foreign Loans. Jefferson, however, felt the government should be under the direction of each state, and all the farmers resented the idea of Foreign Loans and Federal Banks.

※

Hamilton was angry and demanded that Jefferson should be the one to resign if he would not go along with what Washington felt was right.

※

George talked and pleaded with Jefferson and Hamilton to stop this mess of open warfare and remember they were there for the nation, but the two were so headstrong and entirely ignored what Washington had to say about the subject.

George knew with this strife that he would have no choice but to run for a second term. He would not be able to leave the Presidency with such a hot mess going on. Jefferson's actions in trying to undermine Hamilton outright almost caused George to release Jefferson from his cabinet position. He was saved this duty however as Jefferson resigned voluntarily in December 1793.

Foreign and Indian Affairs dogged and plagued Washington as well. April of 1792 saw a time when the French Revolutionary Wars had broken out. It was between France and Great Britain. After George gained the approval of his cabinet, he stepped up and proclaimed the neutrality of America.

Hamilton designed the Jay Treaty to normalize the trade relations they had with Great Britain, get them out of the western forts, and settle the financial debts left over from the Revolution. It was John Jay that negotiated and then signed the Jay Treaty. Washington supported the Treaty, and he was not resistant to criticism from the Republicans. They even accused Washington of taking more than what his yearly pay; he never responded publicly to this accusation. Sometimes it is better to ignore remarks that have no basis than try to respond as it will only make you look guilty.

Anyone who holds a public office must have thick skin as

there will always be someone there ready to tear you down no matter what you do or say. They will be sitting with their cloak and dagger to kick and stab you at anything you try to do for the good.

☙❧

After the treaty had been signed, the United States relations with France started to deteriorate, and this would throw problems in the lap of future President John Adams.

☙❧

For George's second term, George seemed to be re-elected easily, but John Adams became Vice President by seventy-seven to fifty votes.

☙❧

George, even though winning a second term, was criticized by the National Newspaper because of his birthday being celebrated and everyone felt he was starting to appear like a ***"monarchist."***

☙❧

Because of all the criticism, Washington laid low, he came to his inauguration wearing plain clothes and arrived in a plain carriage. His inauguration was held inside the Hall of the Senate Chamber of Congress in Philadelphia. The oath was administered by Associate Justice Cushing. George delivered the shortest inaugural speech ever on record.

☙❧

In 1793, George signed into law the Fugitive Slave Act that would allow the owners of slaves to cross over state lines and bring back their escaped slaves.

※

When he went to Congress to talk to them about foreign treaties, he didn't like the way he was treated. He did not feel he was being treated like a President. He would never consult Congress again on any foreign policy decision. It would set forth what would happen for all future presidents, that they rarely would discuss with Congress before they made any foreign decisions about policy.

※

While Washington was President, two major political battles took place. The first hurdle was when those who had a strict translation of what the Constitution said and then those who opposed. The second dispute that broke out was due to those who favored England and then those who supported France in the European War.

※

The followers who stood for strict Constitutional translation were headed up by no other than Madison. They meant for the government to be no stronger than what had been defined in the Constitution.

※

Then there were the Federalists, that Alexander Hamilton led, that felt the government had powers that were implied over each state. Hamilton even proposed the Federal Government create a Bank of the United States so it would help to fuel economic growth. Madison's group said the government did not have that kind of power from the constitution. George Washington went along with the Federalists and BOOM; there was a Bank built.

※

Secretary of State under Washington was Thomas Jefferson, and he took the side of France who was at war with England. Hamilton took the side of England. Washington stood in the middle.

※

George felt the United States should step back and stay out of Europe's problems and conflicts. He also thought the United States should have peacetime as long as possible so they could increase strength before getting involved in any more wars.

※

Alexander Hamilton had a plan to improve America's economic condition and to pass an excise tax on whiskey. Western Pennsylvania farmers were angry about the tax; they felt it was targeting them. The farmers sold whiskey, and it was an easy way to transport their extra grain over the mountains to the eastern markets.

※

The angered farmers living in the west started protesting the tax the moment it passed in 1791. When 1794 rolled around Congress decided to make some changes, which would include that they would not require farmers to be assessed with any payments according to the law, to come to Philadelphia.

※

At this time, a mandate was issued against 75 of the farmers who Congress believed to be defying the law. A marshall was assigned to serving the farmers. He served all but the very last farmer on the list and his name was Miller, and he was out in the field when the agent came by the farm.

※

Word spread quickly that the agent was in their town and 37 of the farmers took off for the house of the revenue agent who thought this might happen and had posted guards around his home. When the farmers got to his house and would not leave, the soldiers opened fire.

※

Six farmers were wounded and one killed. They disbursed but came back the next day with 500 men. One of the men were killed and the rest burned down the home of the revenue agent who had taken off the night before. It did not take long before 6,000 people marched through Pittsburg as part of the rebellion.

※

When word reached George Washington, he immediately

called for the states to prepare their militia to stop the revolt. Each state sent a total of 15,000 men to Washington's army that he was personally leading. When George and the military had made it to Western Pennsylvania all the rebel rousers had scattered.

※

Ten people were arrested, but they were all pardoned or acquitted. It ended the only armed rebellion until the beginning of the Civil War.

※

One of the more significant events that took place during Washington's term was concluded with a lot of debate but almost no conflict. It was ratifying the first ten amendments of the constitution which we know as the Bill of Rights.

※

George and Martha owned slaves from Africa and those slaves descendants. Martha and George were not personally responsible for the institution of slavery, but since he was the President, after all, he could be found as the one responsible for encouraging and tolerating the act of slavery.

※

It seems from historical research that George considered his slaves not worthy of decent clothes as well as other basic needs of life. You find conflicting reports as to how he treated his slaves. More often than not you will see that the following is what you will uncover. It does not seem to fit the man that we consider as the first President of the United States.

❦

Some authors who will take a stand for George will tell you that he would never take his slave's teeth; so much so that he would pull their teeth to replace his bad teeth with the healthy teeth he had extracted from their mouths. There seems to be much argument and debate over this issue. I for one believe that he did procure his real teeth from the slaves, he might have bought them, but it may have possibly been part of his punishment as he encouraged violence to make his slaves stay in line.

❦

They will go on to tell you that he might have paid them or other slaves that did not work on his plantation for their teeth. He did not pay much for teeth, however. It seems the going rate for teeth was usually two front teeth for a guinea. It is documented in his plantation record books.

❦

It seems there was a dentist in Philadelphia that made George's first set of false teeth and guess where rumors say he got the teeth for his dentures.

❦

George Washington as a slaveholder "***followed***" what they called the "***standards***" that everyone else did with their slaves. George believed and downright encouraged being violent with his slaves as a way to keep them scared and subservient to him. It has been said that he sold and bought his slaves only for economic reasons. Of course, because of this, it would sometimes separate families. He made sure while he was President that his slaves did not learn about their right to freedom. If he was able to do all of this, I say he would take their teeth to those who think that George would never be a part of that practice.

※

For George's entire life he had trouble with his teeth, and it seems that the historians have researched issues with his teeth extensively. At age 22 he lost his first adult tooth, and by the time he was president he had only one tooth left. A dentist by the name of John Greenwood made him four sets of false teeth, and while he was President, he went through several sets.

※

Because of his dental issues, he was in constant pain, and he took a lot of laudanum (today it is a controlled opioid drug), which Tobias Lear would seek out for him. (One has also to wonder if he was hooked on this drug as well.

※

He didn't just have slaves at Mount Vernon; he had them while he was President at his Presidential home. He selflessly supported liberty for white people but opposed freedom for the Blacks.

※

While Martha and George were living in Philadelphia, there were some of their slaves who worked around the President's home. Others were made to live in the slave quarters, which were just five feet from the entrance of what is now called the Liberty Bell Center. What irony?

※

It seems George was a great leader as a President, a general, and a patriot. His greatness did not overflow to caring for his slaves – especially when it came to the terms of how they existed or in regards to their clothing, food, health, and shelter. Several of the slaves had to rummage for old burlap bags to wear for their outer garments because George would not dress them appropriately.

※

George could be caught in a lie when it came to owning slaves. On December 19th, 1786, he made a vow that he would never purchase another slave. It did not matter, he accepted slaves as a form of payment on a debt and bought them to work on some renovations at Mount Vernon.

※

Those he brought to Philadelphia he treated in a demeaning, degrading, debasing, and dehumanizing manner. The nine he brought with him to Philadelphia suffered so much that two of his favorites – Oney and Hercules Judge – escaped as well as two more – Christopher and Richmond Sheets. At Mount Vernon, while he was away, seven left, although they did not live in freedom for long as George had them hunted down and brought back.

❦

While George was serving his first term in office, the political parties were starting to emerge. Alexander Hamilton wanted a Federalist Party, and Thomas Jefferson wanted the Democratic-Republicans.

❦

If you visited the President's Home while it was in the temporary capitals before it was decided that its forever home would be Washington, D.C. you would find Martha had warm hospitality that always made her guests feel comfortable.

❦

Martha did not like high society and the "***formal compliments and all the empty ceremonies***" that went with that group. Martha only cared about what came from someone's heart. Abigail Adams always praised her and knew that Martha was one of those genuine people who created esteem and love in others.

❦

When George first began his Presidency, they rented a house on Broadway, and it also served as his office. It exposed Martha to all of George's visitors, and because of that it drew Martha into political discussions more than she would have ever been involved in had George's office and home been separated.

❦

When the seat of the new government moved to Philadelphia, the Washingtons moved into a house on High Street, and Martha's entertaining started to become more elaborate. Martha was careful and would not take any stands on public issues, and this caused her to be criticized.

Some of the people attacked her for the fact that they felt she was entertaining on too large a scale and much too opulent for a Republican government.

When George was nearing the end of his second term, it seemed he could do nothing right for the people. They were critical about his past successes, and they felt he had Federalists leanings. They even accused him of being greedy and ambitious.

It was such a massive shift to the man that they had laid flowers at this feet, held parades, and cried over when he came into town for his first inauguration.

He started to feel that the press was out to get him because a lot of what they printed was nothing but falsehoods. He even expressed the same in his farewell address as to how troubled he felt about the backbiting and lying that came from the press.

His Farewell address did not help calm people. Instead, they became angrier.

When it was time for George to retire after his second term of office was over Martha was too glad to go back to Mount Vernon and some peace and quiet.

❧ XI ☙
GEORGE AND GOD

"Liberty, when it begins to take root, is a plant of rapid growth."

— GEORGE WASHINGTON

❁

When you try to find out about George's religious beliefs, you will find how difficult it is to come up with absolute conclusions. It seems that George has been reviewed in different lights all the way from being a Deist to a believing, practicing Christian. This author and researcher, however, believes he was a practicing Christian.

❁

But no matter what the conclusion seems to be, there seems

to be a common thread about Washington's view with religion.

❧

Washington was found as a devoted member in the Anglican Church. It was in 1762 when he became a vestryman who oversaw the affairs for the Pohick Church in Truro Parish. He also served as churchwarden for three terms, (however long their terms were), in helping care for the poor.

❧

It seems that church attendance for George varied during his lifetime. We must remember he was away at war for several years and therefore could not bring the war to a halt to run home to church. It seems that history wants to claim his attendance got better during his Presidency. It does not indicate that it was more during his second term when the newspapers were hounding him constantly or not. There was one prior pastor at Pohick that said he had never known a more faithful attendant at church as George.

❧

Regarding his spirituality, George was one of those people who was just quiet about his religion. It is reported that George would conduct his prayer sessions in private. His nephew witnessed his Uncle George during his personal times of devotions with his Bible open and kneeled every morning and every evening.

❧

Many Christians seek quietness and solitude to pray and speak to their God. It is an individual's choice.

※

It has been said that Washington refused to take part in communion, but there seem to be some conflicting reports on this issue. One of the stories says that George participated in Communion before he was the leader of the Continental Army.

※

After coming back from the army, it became his practice to leave the church before communion would take place and leave Martha there to partake. It has also been said that the assistant rector in Philadelphia of the Christ Church got on to him for leaving. How do we know that maybe his conscience bothered him for having killed so many while at war and he felt he could no longer take Communion? Whatever the reason, it was his reason and no one else's business.

※

Some question as to whether George was one that believed in Heaven or the afterlife. There is a reference in some of his writings about there being a coming judgment, and that one day in the future of meeting with "***the Creator.***" Remember he was a Freemason and their tenets require that you believe in Heaven and the afterlife.

※

When his step-daughter Patsy died, he prayed for God to bring her back as she lay dying.

❦

When you look at Washington's beliefs about God, it is not hard to figure out that he did believe in God the Creator of some sort. The God he believed in seemed to have three main traits; he was inscrutable, wise, and irresistible. George seemed to refer to God by several names, but the one he used most was "***Providence.***" Sometimes he used the Creator God. It seems George thought and believed that people were not just passing through this world. Whatever happened to someone was by the will of Providence.

❦

Washington did feel that God was instrumental when the United States was developed. It seems that armed with these facts; he believed in a God that is continuously influencing all the happenings around us every day.

❦

Research does not tell us he was a devout Christian. The only mention of Jesus Christ is in public papers. It may mean nothing however as it may have been the practice of the day by the Episcopalians or Anglicans of that time.

❧ XII ☙
NO LOOKING BACK – ON TO MT. VERNON

"The Constitution is the guide which I never will abandon."

— GEORGE WASHINGTON

※

When George finally retired from his Presidency, and he and Martha made it back to Mount Vernon it was with sheer relief. He worked and devoted a lot of time to his plantations, his distillery, and his business interests. His distillery made its first batch of spirits in 1797. Of all his plantation operations none of them were making any money. He was losing money quickly just at Mount Vernon because of his unproductive slaves. It was like a hole in a bag of marbles with the way money was running out it.

When 1798 rolled around, the relations of the United States and France had before were deteriorating so much that war was unavoidable. Shockingly, George accepted and did serve as a senior officer in the United States Army until his death. George could be found planning in meetings for emergencies that might arise but avoided any involvement with the fine details. Most of the work he delegated to Hamilton and that included the active leadership. George never returned to field duty.

Most people in America thought he was rich because of where he lived and how much he owned. His wealth was tied up in slaves and land. It has been estimated that he was worth about $1 million in dollars of that day and that would be equivalent to about $21 million today. His money was in his land and holdings, but it was not liquid, there was no cash available due to this fact unless he sold some of his holdings.

It began on December 12, 1799, when George was out riding on a horse around his plantation. It was freezing rain, hailing, and snowing. He and Martha had guests coming that evening, and he did not want to keep them waiting, so he went to eat supper and did not change out of his wet clothes.

The next day the weather got even worse, and the snow got much heavier. George had a very sore throat, and he walked through the snow down the hill to mark trees that he had decided should be cleared. When he got home that evening, his chest was feeling very congested and was getting hoarse, but he was still in a good mood.

※

Around 3:00 a.m. he woke up because he was having great difficulty breathing and could barely speak or swallow. George was a firm believer in bloodletting, so he had Albin Rawlins to take about a pint of his blood.

※

At this point, Martha had Tobias call the second doctor to the home. It was a Dr. Gustavus Brown. Dr. Craik came at nine that morning and made a blister on George's throat to balance out Geroge's fluids in his body. Craik bled Washington again and then commanded that a potion be made of sage tea and vinegar for George to gargle. It was eleven o'clock, and Dr. Brown had not arrived yet, so Craik sent for another doctor. At noon they gave George an enema, but it seemed not to have any effect on George. They then bled George for what was to be the fourth time. It was later revealed that with the last bleeding they took thirty-two ounces of blood. When they were finished with him over half of his blood had been taken from him. Dr. Craik gave an emetic so George would vomit and again it did not serve any benefit.

※

At four-thirty that afternoon, George wanted Martha to come near to him so he could talk to her and asked her to bring his two wills from his office. When he reviewed them, he threw one away, and Martha went immediately and burned it.

※

George then asked for Tobias Lear. He told Tobias that he knew he was dying and then gave Tobias some instructions about some of his business.

※

At five George got up from his bed, got dressed, and went to sit in his chair. Within thirty minutes he went back to bed. George thanked all three doctors for trying their best. At eight that evening Dr. Craik attempted more blisters, and even poultices were applied to George's legs and arms. One doctor wanted to do an emergency tracheotomy which MIGHT have saved his life, but the other two doctors said no. George finally told them to stop trying; he knew he was going to die. George told his Doctor that he died hard, but that he was not afraid to die.

※

His death came quickly and for sure unexpectedly. For his final instructions, he said to bury him decently and wait three days before putting him in the vault. The last words he ever uttered was "***Tis well.***" Martha sat at the foot of his bed calmly composed. George died a peaceful death at 10:00 p.m. December 14, 1799. George's Masonic Lodge took care of the funeral and the arrangements. When the news made it to Washington, D.C., Congress immediately closed for the rest of the day. The next morning the chair of the Speaker was veiled in black.

※

Four days later the funeral was held at Mount Vernon where they were to inter his body. The Foot Soldiers and Cavalry lead the entire procession, while six other Colonels that had served for Washington at the time of the revolution served as George's pallbearers. The funeral itself was only for family and friends. Congress had chosen Henry Lee III to give the Eulogy.

※

In December 1800, Congress passed a bill to build a mausoleum that would cost $200,000. The measure was defeated by the Southern Senators and Representatives because they opposed the entire plan and thought George's body should stay at Mount Vernon.

※

Martha wore black for one year to signify she was still in mourning for her George. It was at this time that Martha went through and burned all the letters that she and George had written to each other to protect their privacy. It seems that only five letters have survived.

※

Martha also released all the slaves that she and George had owned and gave them their freedom.

❦

Martha was depressed after George passed away and she quit eating and wasted away. Martha came down with a high fever of 105.3, developed heart failure and death overtook her at age 70 on May 22, 1802.

❦

They are both buried at Mount Vernon, and neither of them has extravagant tombstones.

❧ XIII ☙
STRENGTHS

※

As a President, he was remarkably orderly, systematic, and solitious (This is a good quality for anyone in any area of your life. To have these characteristics will serve you well through your entire life. Never be a sloth or a slob. It can only slow you down.)

※

He tried to involve his staff in making Presidential decisions (Remember, there is no "***I***" in Team. The more heads put together is better than one and others may come up with ideas or had experiences in the past that may help you solve a problem or know someone who has had more experience in the field that you can talk to about the issue to allow your venture to be a success on any decision.)

❧

His first year as President he could do no wrong and brought the country together.

❧

When he would set a goal for himself, or a vision he always worked until it was obtained (George never gave up, he kept on trying no matter what he was faced with and this is to be admired. A good lesson for anyone in life; to never accept defeat.)

❧

He assumed a leadership role as a soldier for which he had no formal training; he was just thrown into the position, and he had to learn by the seat of his pants. (He made the best out of the situation and as always, learned from his mistakes. He made many in the role of a soldier, but he knew not to remake some of the mistakes he had made before.)

❧

George always learned from his mistakes (This invariably is a good quality for everyone to pursue. If you cannot learn from your mistakes, you will never advance and gain any of your goals in life.)

⚜ XIV ⚜
WEAKNESSES

George seemed to be a whiner and a backstabber when it came to wanting to move up in his career military wise.

※

George gave away locks of his hair to admiring women.

※

He was a bit what you would call cocky as he would go against the orders of his superiors and it caused problems, some problems that cost the lives of soldiers.

※

He had written a letter to a married woman letting her know

he loved her while he was engaged to Martha. He must have thought of her all the time while he was married to Martha because after his Presidency he still wrote her again saying that everything he had accomplished in his life has not been able to make me forget the happiest moments of my life which I enjoyed in your company. (Shame on him.)

George was a careless soldier at the beginning of his career as a soldier. He never thought things through.

He loved being noticed, and he would do anything for attention.

At election time he would fill voters up with beer, hard cider, brandy, wine, and rice punch too as much as 170 gallons to buy their votes.

He was a snob in many ways as he never wanted to be around anyone that was beneath his status.

He cheated veterans of the French/Indian War for their land. He deceived them badly. Some were glad to get the money, and others realized how badly they had been duped.

He was terrible at public speaking (he never spoke where you could hear him, and he did not keep up with what was going on now if it did not involve war.)

※

He lost more battles than he ever won.

✣ XV ✤
CONCLUSION

༺༻

No matter whether the person you study is alive today or they were alive 200 – 300 years ago, no matter how hard you try you will never know everything there is to know about that person.

༺༻

I say this because George Washington was a quiet man and most quiet people, you must draw out of them what they have on their minds and then you never know what is going on inside their brain. Those who are talkative creatures you will usually know them from their toes to the top of their heads.

༺༻

I think there was a lot more to George Washington than what can be found in any of the books dedicated to him.

※

I think he was a man who always wanted biological children but knew that would never happen. It seems he was also a big flirt with women when Martha was not around. It seems he spent a lot of time smiling and encouraging their glances in his direction. It appeared he glowed when other women would look at him arduously. He would go so far as to clip locks of his hair and send it to women who would request it.

※

When you study George closely, it seems that he never had a real sense of confidence in anything that he did or started to do, but he always learned from his mistakes.

※

No matter what, it took a lot of nerve to be able to step out and serve the people of this great country as the first President of the United States and play everything by ear knowing that you were setting a precedence of what was to come for all future generations.

※

I am not writing this book to "***run down***" George Washington. I wrote this book to show that even great people have flaws. We are all human, and in some way, we are all flawed. It is to be expected as none of us are perfect.

༺༻

Just because he was considered the "***Father of our Country***" does not mean he was ever a perfect man. He had his strengths and weaknesses, and he wanted so badly to be known for something. All the while he was making history, he never realized it and craved for more.

༺༻

More good books you may want to read about George Washington:

༺༻

- Washington – A Life - by Ron Chernow
- His Excellency – George Washington – by Joseph J. Ellis
- George Washington, First Guardian of America – by Michael Crawley

YOUR FREE EBOOK!

As a way of saying thank you for reading our book, we're offering you a free copy of the below eBook.

Happy Reading!

GO WWW.THEHISTORYHOUR.COM/CLEO/

Made in the USA
San Bernardino, CA
09 March 2020